For Fergus — M.M.
For Rosie and her friends in Miss Bailey's class — A.W.

First published as 'Take a Walk on a Rainbow'
in Great Britain in 1999 by Macdonald Young Books,

This edition published in 2009 by Wayland,
an imprint of Hachette Children's Books,
338 Euston Road, London NW1 3BH
www.hachettelivre.co.uk

Commissioning Editor Dereen Taylor
Editor Rosie Nixon
Designer Liz Black
Science and Language Consultant Dr Carol Ballard

Text © Miriam Moss
Illustrations © Amanda Wood
Volume © Macdonald Young Books 1999
Little Bees artwork © Clare Mackie

Moss, Miriam
  A rainbow of colours: a first look at colour.
  (Little Bees)
  1. Colours - Juvenile Literature
  I. Title
  535.6

Printed in China by WKT Co. Ltd.

ISBN 978 07502 5846 3

A Rainbow
of
Colours

A Rainbow of Colours

by Miriam Moss
Illustrated by Amanda Wood

WAYLAND

Storm clouds gather and the sky turns black.

6

When there's no light there's no colour.

CRACK! Lightning flashes

8

and Tilly's room lights up with colour.

made up of all the colours of the rainbow.

This makes the sunlight spread out into all the colours of the rainbow.

13

The colours of the lights show us

Watch out Grandad!

14

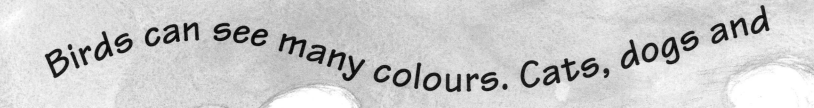

Birds can see many colours. Cats, dogs and

Do you think that birds and animals see colours like we do?

Well that bird can see those red berries!

horses only see in black, white and grey.

The bright red colour of the

A poisonous frog warns the monkey not to eat it.

27

28

fades and everything looks black and grey again.

29

Mix it up!

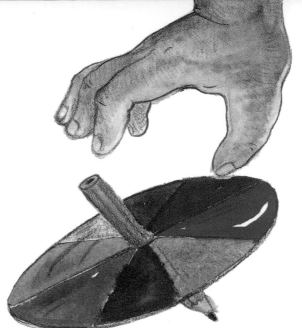

The light that shines from the sun looks white, but it's really made up of all the colours of the rainbow.

See for yourself when you spin this simple colour wheel. All the colours will mix together and look white before your eyes!

To make the wheel:

1 Cut out a circle of card

2 Colour it like this:

3 Stick a pencil through the middle.

4 Spin it!

Useful words

Chameleon
A small lizard living in hot countries. A chameleon can hide by changing its skin to the same colour as the things around it.

Lightning
Giant flashes of light that break out of thunder clouds during a storm. You can see the lightning flash before you hear the sound of thunder.

Rainbow
An arch in the sky made of lots of colours. A rainbow appears when white light from the sun shines through raindrops in the air. The raindrops make the white light spread out into all the colours of the rainbow.

Storm
Bad weather. There can be strong winds, rain or snow and sometimes thunder and lightning.